Get Your House Clean Now:
The Home Cleaning Method
Anyone Can Master

BETH MCGEE

Copyright 2015 Beth McGee
All Rights Reserved
ISBN: 0692615237
ISBN-13: 978-0692615232

This book is dedicated to all of the people
who have trusted me to care for their homes.

Special Thanks to:
Nora Hardy, Editor
and
Thor Svartefoss, Cover Designer
thorsvartefoss.com

DISCLAIMER

Disclaimer- While attempts have been made to verify the information provided in this publication, neither the author nor the publisher assumes any responsibility for errors, omissions, or contrary interpretations of the subject matter herein. This book is for entertainment and informational purposes only. The views expressed are those of the author alone and should not be taken as expert instruction or commands. The reader is responsible for his or her own actions. Neither the author nor the publisher assumes any responsibility or liability whatsoever on behalf of the purchaser or reader of these materials. The reader is responsible for their own use of any products or methods mentioned in this publication.

This book includes information about products and equipment offered by third parties. As such, the author does not assume responsibility or liability for any third party products or opinions. Third party product manufacturers have not sanctioned this book, nor does the author receive any compensation from said manufacturers for sharing information regarding their products.

CONTENTS

Thank You

About the Author

INTRODUCTION

Welcome! I'm so glad you've chosen my book, *Get Your House Clean Now: The Home Cleaning Method Anyone Can Master*. There are so many books about cleaning and I'm grateful you've chosen mine. I hope you will find the information here as useful as I have. It has taken me 20 years as a business owner, working in the field, to perfect this process.

Being in comfortable and inviting spaces can enhance our life experience and make us feel good about ourselves and the choices we make. When you finish this book, you will know how to get your home clean in the most efficient way for excellent results, so you can enjoy your spaces as much as possible. This isn't a seven day or 30 day course on getting your home clean. This book will prepare you to get your house clean right now.

Cleaning may not come naturally to you. So often, we don't have good examples to teach us how to do it. Don't be disappointed in yourself for not having the knack for it. It is the rare bird who actually enjoys cleaning, but we can work together to make it tolerable, and even enjoyable, once you see the results of your efforts.

For the last 20 years, I've owned a hospitality business: one in which I clean and prepare homes for their owner's arrival after a long day, a week's vacation, or winter abroad. I've turned over lake-front cottages for weekly rental, prepared large homes and estates for posh parties and other events, cared for large properties and estates in the absence of their owners, and tidied up the smallest of modest homes and apartments for residents who just love to be at ease in their homes during their down time. Each of these experiences has given me an opportunity to develop and master the best strategies for achieving excellent results.

Many clients have become more confident and prepared to care for their own home, once I've gotten it into shape for a good, fresh start. I have shared with them the instructions you will find in this book. Many have asked for a manual of this method, so finally I have created one. Many have found these techniques offer them a new outlook on their own ability to care for their home and of cleaning in general.

Whether you want to clean your humble abode to enjoy your spaces, start your own cleaning business, prepare your home to rent on vacation rental sites like Airbnb.com and Homeaway.com, or help your house cleaner work most effectively for you, this book will help you do it. I will provide you with a lifetime of knowledge to help you care for your own spaces and enjoy your time in them.

In this book, you will find great information beyond the normal copied and pasted cleaning tips you may have seen a million times on the Internet. It is my intention to leave you feeling confident about your skills in this area, and looking forward to sharing your home as a host or simply savoring the peace of your own clean and lovely spaces. Let's get started!

With gratitude,

Beth McGee

2015

A CLEAN HOME

Before you can live comfortably in your spaces, or stage your home for guests and potential buyers, it's important to get serious about cleaning. When you walk into a hotel room while away on holiday, you don't expect to see mold, or water stains, or grime or messes on the floor. You expect that someone has paid close attention to the cleanliness of your room. Why shouldn't you expect to live in similar conditions? Conditions where you know your spaces are clean and safe and always ready to receive guests with just a quick touch-up. Conditions like these enhance your social life and satisfy your mother, or just plain give you a lovely place to call home.

Sure, your home isn't a five-star hotel, and the expectations might not be quite the same, but you deserve clean spaces. If you can't afford to hire someone, this book will help you get your place into shape and maintain it easily.

To begin, it's important to be in the right mindset. Don't look at the messes in your home as they loom over you, thinking "How am I ever going to get this done?" Instead, know that each step you take will bring you closer to a routine that comes naturally, and soon you'll be cleaning it like a pro.

There are so many cleaning products to choose from. So often, they don't accomplish the task they say they will on the label. It's rare to find a product that does what it claims. This wastes time and money. I will only share with you the products that have proved themselves to me over the last twenty years.

I will not waste your time by only suggesting "all-natural" cleaners for tough jobs, but there are a couple of options for regular maintenance that work well and are inexpensive. Keep in mind, using vinegar is a so-so choice for some cleaning jobs, but it isn't going to get tough jobs done. Neither is baking soda. Each serves a purpose, but I will leave that to you and Google to figure out. I won't be addressing them here.

There are only a few products you really need, but you will also need tools to get the job done. Don't be afraid to make the investment. Your job will be so much easier if you make the initial investment and have what you need, rather than trying to make do, which causes you to work harder. If

your toolbox consists of the tools I mention in this
book, you will work smarter and faster.

CLEANING PRODUCT GUIDE

In appreciation of your readership, a complimentary Cleaning Product Guide is available at:

www.bethmcgeebooks.com/clean-product-guide

The text of this book mentions a Product Guide several times that may be found at the above link. This Product Guide may be used to recognize and/or order any or all of the products and tools mentioned in this book.

Thank you, dear reader.

CLEANING TOOLS

To clean your home efficiently, you will need the right tools. This is a list of the must-haves, as well as some items that make it easier to do the work if you choose to use them.

Vacuum Cleaner

A vacuum cleaner, preferably a canister with an electric power head, is the only acceptable tool for cleaning the dirt off your floors, walls, and ceilings to enjoy real cleanliness. If you have hard floors throughout your home, you don't necessarily need a vacuum with an electric power head unless you have area rugs, but you will need a vacuum with a minimum of 12 AMPS to complete the job well. The electric power head is important, as the alternative is a power head powered by suction.

These are not efficient. If the suction is low, it won't brush dirt up effectively or suck up the dirt once it's brushed out of the rug. If the suction is too high, the power head will often cling to the floor, not allowing anything to get vacuumed up, and possibly stopping the brushes from spinning altogether. An electric power head will remain spinning and removing dirt as long as you haven't vacuumed up something that clogs the vacuum inlet or gets wrapped around the brushes until they stop.

I have high standards for a vacuum cleaner. To be efficient and cost effective, the perfect vacuum must:

* Have a motor that is 12 AMPS or more
* Have attachments that are housed on the vacuum
* Have an electric power head that is easily removable by step-release

* Have a long wand for reaching under furniture and high spaces (preferably telescoping, but not imperative)
* Have a cord at least 20 feet long (the longer, the better)
* Be easy to pull around
* Have a HEPA filter (great, but not imperative)
* Have controls on the handle
* Be under $200

I have used many brands, from Kenmore®, Shark®, Miele® and Hoover®, Oreck®, Dyson®, Electrolux®, Kirby®, and more. I can only highly recommend two brands after two decades of using them all.

First, the Kenmore® canister vacuum is the best quality for the money. I have used Kenmore® canister vacuum cleaners for the 20 years I've been in business. These vacuums have cleaned an average of 10 homes a week and lasted many years at that pace. I have used the most expensive models and the cheaper models and I find the lower end models work extremely well and offer the highest quality for the money. Kenmore® has a model with an electric power head that is generally below $200. If you watch for sales, you can get one for a little over $100. The vacuum bags that offer the best quality for the money for this type of vacuum are made by Arm & Hammer™ and are available online or at big-box stores. This brand in particular has met my stress tests. The bags don't rip, they fit the vacuum well, and they are low odor, which keeps the vacuum and your room from smelling bad.

Second, Shark® makes a great light-weight vacuum that's easy to store and has many of the features that meet my requirements. The Shark Rocket® is a terrific bagless model, so no extra expense for regular use. It's easy to use and has a great power head for a small vacuum. It's not too heavy and gets to all of the places you need in order to make your home as clean as possible. It also has many attachments. It runs between $100-200 and it's available at stores that often offer 20% off coupons so watch for those deals!

The takeaway here is that you need a quality vacuum. A vacuum that allows you to reach under furniture and in high places. It must be below $200 to be economical and must meet the criteria above for most efficiency and quality. You will not regret making this purchase if you want a clean home. Remember, "most expensive" does not mean best quality. In fact, in my experience, the most expensive vacuums are over-hyped, inefficient, and don't live up to many of their claims. (Save your money for sipping margaritas by the shore!)

You will likely be able to order Kenmore® vacuums online for a long time, even if you don't have a Sears store near you. I hope they will continue to do business for many years to come, as they are a steadfast American retail institution, but I don't want to be unrealistic and pin your hopes on a product that won't be available when you read this. If you are unable to find a Kenmore® or Shark Rocket® vacuum as I've described here at the time of this writing, try to find a canister vacuum with as many of the specifications I've listed as possible.

A good vacuum will last you a long time and do great work for you if you treat it well. To see the model I use, or ones I recommend, visit the Product Guide online for the latest information. The models I recommend will do what you need and more.

Other Tools

Bucket (2.5 gallon is a good size)

Microfiber cloths- May be purchased in bundles of 10 or more at big box building and discount stores, often in the automotive section.

Feather duster- for light dusting of intricate spaces as well as quick touch-ups between thorough cleanings.

Scotchbrite® scratch-free sponges

Large plastic cup (approx. 32 oz) for rinsing tubs

Stainless steel pot scrubber

Rubber gloves- Do not think you won't need rubber gloves. Your work will go much more quickly when you remove the "ick" factor from touching unpleasant messes.

Twist mop- A mop that has a removable string mop head that can be taken off and washed in a linen bag. (Note: it must be put in a linen bag in order to wash in the machine because it will become tangled and unusable if you don't.) It allows you to wring the mop out with each dip in the bucket. This is NOT the wring mop that has Handi-wipe type strips hanging from it. Nor is it a microfiber twist mop. The common brand I have had great success with is a Libman® Tornado mop. If you do not have this brand locally, search online or find one similar in style in your area. I DO NOT recommend using a sponge mop. Sponge mops will not get your floors clean. They will push the dirt around and grind it further into your floor.

Twist mop alternative- O-Cedar™ Ultra-Max mop and bucket kit.-This mop is terrific. It is a flat pad that is removable and washable. It collects dirt well and cleans floors effectively. The bucket has a squeeze mechanism that wrings the water out for a lightly damp mop. Snap-off replacement pads are inexpensive to have on hand in case one is dirty.

Mesh linen bag- Wash your twist mop head in a mesh linen bag to keep it from getting tangled and becoming unusable.

CLEANING PRODUCTS

You will waste so much time in your life trying new "amazing" products that brag about their spectacular results. If I had every dollar back for every product I tested and was disappointed by, I would be a wealthy woman.

Luckily for you, I've wasted *my* money and *my* time and now I'm able to share with you the best products to get the job done well with the least amount of effort. Why would you want to do more work than you have to? I'll share why I like each product and the ways you can use them.

After twenty years, I've used nearly every product on the shelves, and have stirred up countless "natural" homemade cleaners found on the Internet. I've even re-tested several to see if their formula had changed enough to be as useful as the ones I've had success with. The products I share with you in this chapter are the best at what I need them to do every day for great results, so these are the only ones I'm going to recommend. You are free to experiment with whichever products you wish.

I receive no compensation from product manufacturers for the information I provide about the products listed in this book. I get the satisfaction that I'm actually helping you save time and money, and get great results. Most other cleaning guides list a bunch of products generically or try to convince you that vinegar is the answer to all of your problems. You won't find that here. What you will find is no BS information for the purpose of making your life easier.

I realize some products may not be available in all areas. But seriously, we have the Internet now. These products can be purchased at any popular online retailer or cleaning supply store, so you can create your very own cleaning product kit to keep on hand. You may want to purchase more than one of each if your home needs a thorough cleaning. You will likely use a lot of product your first time around. After that, these products should last you much longer with simple, regularly scheduled cleanings.

Throughout this book, product names will be in **bold** for easy recognition.

Product List

Bar Keeper's Friend®- This is a non-scratch scrubbing powder in a gold shaker container. It is *not* Bon Ami. That is a different product that doesn't work nearly as well for the purposes described in this book. Bar Keeper's Friend® will not scratch your surfaces and cleans amazingly well. I no longer use Comet or Ajax because they can scratch and have a strong odor. Follow the instructions on the can and you will be pleasantly surprised at how much work Bar Keeper's Friend® does for you. It's also safe on glass and ceramic cook-tops when using a scratch-free sponge or cloth.

Scrub Free® Bathroom Cleaner with Oxi-Clean™ (Not Scrub Free® with Bleach)- This cleaner is for tubs, showers, fixtures, toilets, and sinks of all sort. I primarily use it in bathrooms because it cleans soap scum and hard water residue off shower walls, doors, and tubs incredibly well with hardly any scrubbing. If you have a really bad tub/shower, a few applications of this product may make it look new, or close to it. The scent is not overwhelming. It shines up kitchen fixtures and sinks as well.

Grease-cutting dish soap such as Dawn® or Palmolive®- There are so many uses for dish soap, full strength or diluted in water, that I can't list them all here. Got a mess or stain that involves grease? This product is your friend. It is my go-to for stove cleaning, can be used to remove grease stains from clothing, or even your outdoor grill. Be sure to have it on hand.

Liquid Gold®- This product is a furniture cleaner, but it has many other uses. After many years of struggling to find a solution for making stainless steel appliances shine, I finally found it in this product. It will also make oiled bronze or brushed nickel fixtures like bathroom handles and shower heads, as well as door knobs and much more, look brand new. **Liquid Gold®** can make your wood furniture look beautiful if you treat it once every few months.

Bleach spray cleaner, such as Clorox® Cleanup® or Scrub Free with Bleach®- Excellent for light colored counter tops and sinks, as well as tough stains on other bleach-safe surfaces. Be cautious of clothing and other items that might be damaged when using this product.

Disinfectant all-purpose liquid cleaner, such as Lysol® All-Purpose Cleaner- This can be used on many floor surfaces and for bathroom/kitchen cleaning as well.

Glass cleaner, such as Glass Plus® or Windex® - I prefer **Glass Plus®** because it has a nice scent, but **Windex®** works well, too. You can use this for windows, kitchen surfaces and walls, light switches, doors, mirrors, etc.

White vinegar- Perfect for washing shower curtain liners in the washing machine and for cleaning glass. It may be diluted in water to clean wood floors. It can also be mixed with lemon juice and dish-soap for a terrific surface cleaner. (See instructions below.)

Homemade Cleaner- Best for maintaining your home once it's clean, fill a spray bottle with 1/2 cup of vinegar, 1/4 cup of lemon juice, and 1/4 cup **Dawn**® dish-soap. This cleaner works for grease-covered stoves, counter tops, sinks, microwaves, bathtubs and shower stalls, and even diluted at 2 TBSP per bucket of water for mopping floors. This all-purpose cleaner is inexpensive to make and cleans very well. Plus, it has a fresh scent. This cleaner is also great for regular maintenance once a deep cleaning has been achieved.

Lime-Away® Toilet Bowl Cleaner- If you have terrible water stains in your toilet, tub, sink, etc…this product may help with a quick fix to get them into shape for regular cleanings with gentler products. Not to be confused with **Lime-Away® Spray Cleaner, Lime-Away® Toilet Bowl Cleaner** is in a container with a spout like other toilet bowl cleaners. It has a gel consistency and is very powerful at removing lime and rust build-up.

If you apply it to the toilet bowl and let it sit for a few minutes, deposits will practically wash away. You may need a couple of applications to get everything looking spiffy. Use at your own risk. Test a small area before using on the entire surface.

Lime-Away® Spray Cleaner- This is a different product than the toilet bowl product mentioned previously. If you have faucet fixtures that have become crusted with lime and water stains or rust, you may have success with this spray cleaner. Read the label to determine if the finish on your fixtures is safe to use this product on.

Goo Gone® Grout Cleaner- This product does an amazing job of cleaning grout on tile floors that have gotten dark with dirt. Let sit for two minutes and nearly every spec of dirt scrubs off easily with a light scrub brush. I have not had success with it removing mold and mildew stains on shower grout, although the label indicates it is good for this purpose.

Resolve® Stain Remover- Hands down, *the best* stain remover out there for removing tough stains like berries, wine, coffee, etc from fabrics and carpets. If you bother with any other brands, you are wasting your time and money.

Out of this long list, the primary cleaners you will need to get started cleaning your home are the following:

* Bar Keeper's Friend®
* Scrub Free® Bathroom Cleaner with Oxi-Clean™
* Dish Soap
* Bleach Spray Cleaner (if you have light counters or sinks that are stained)
* Glass Cleaner

* Disinfectant All Purpose Cleaner (Lysol)
* Lime-Away® Toilet Bowl Cleaner (if you have difficult hard water stains)
* Lime-Away® Spray Cleaner (if you have hard water stains)
* Homemade Cleaner

If you wish to get your home clean with the least amount of effort, do not scrimp on this list. This is the bare minimum you will need to get the job done. To make things easier, I've put together a free Product Guide to help you order the right products and tools to make getting started that much easier. The Product Guide may be found at **www.bethmcgeebooks.com/clean-product-guide**

Let's get to work, shall we?

CLEANING OVERVIEW

In the following section, I will share with you the routine that I've perfected over the past 20 years in my cleaning business. This routine is thorough and efficient, and can help you achieve excellent results. Using this method with the tools and products I've shared, I manage deep cleanings thoroughly and quickly, as well as provide ongoing maintenance with ease.

As I describe my process throughout this book, I assume your home is a mess that hasn't been cleaned in a while, has stuck on food, stains, soap scum, etc… and will need a really thorough first cleaning. If this describes your home, be patient and get ready to work. Please note that this is the same routine I use once a home is clean and ready to be maintained on a regular basis, which is most often every other week. You could push it to monthly, but waiting that long may diminish your quality of life experience there, and cause you to work much harder at each cleaning. Bathrooms and kitchens are harder to get clean the longer you wait in between cleanings, and who wants to walk around their floors tracking dog hair and food crumbs all over for weeks on end? Never underestimate the power of a clean home.

A brief rundown of my routine looks like this:

1. Kitchen
2. Living Spaces
3. Bedrooms
4. Bathrooms
5. Floors

We begin in the kitchen, so put on those rubber gloves and....Ready? Set. Go!

KITCHEN

Turn on all available lighting when cleaning to be sure to catch areas where messes may be hiding.

Fill the sink with hot tap water and add a dollop of grease-cutting dish soap. Use this sink water to complete many kitchen cleaning tasks. Rinse and wring out a microfiber cloth in the dish water as often as it gets dirty. If the kitchen needs a thorough cleaning, empty the dish water and refill the sink with fresh water and dish soap as needed.

Remove grates or burner guards from a gas stove and put them in the sink to soak. Electric stove burners that pop up and unplug from the stove can be taken out if removable to clean the trays beneath them. These burner trays may be soaked in the sink if they are removable. Electric burners should not be placed in water.

Dishwasher

If the dishwasher has a removable filter, take it out and soak it in clean, soapy water for several minutes and come back to it. Move on to other cleaning until the filter is clean and ready to replace in the dishwasher. Once the filter is back in place, pour 1 cup of white vinegar on the bottom of the dishwasher and run on a cycle for heavy duty cleaning. It should sparkle once the cycle is complete. If your dishwasher has a door gasket, try **Bar Keeper's Friend**® to remove mold stains and rinse. If it needs more attention after rinsing, try **bleach spray cleaner** and rinse with a clean microfiber cloth when finished.

Microwave and/or Toaster Oven

If there is a microwave above the stove, clean it before cleaning the stove top. Remove and wash the tray. Clean the inside of the microwave with a damp microfiber cloth. Most everything should come off with just hot soapy water, but tougher stains can be washed away with **Homemade Cleaner**. If it has a white interior and there are food stains inside, **bleach spray cleaner** may help remove them. Do not ever use an abrasive in the microwave. If the interior is stainless steel and there are racks inside, these may be cleaned with soapy water, but tougher stains can be scrubbed away easily with **Bar Keeper's Friend**® and a **scratch-free sponge**. When finished, wipe down the outside with **glass cleaner**.

If your toaster oven has a drip tray, remove it and throw away the crumbs. Wash it in the sink with a dab of **undiluted dish soap**. This should take the grease off. For burned on stains, use **Bar Keeper's Friend**®. To avoid future stains, apply a layer of aluminum foil to the tray and fold the longer edges underneath. Inexpensive non-stick, heat-resistant toaster oven tray liners that wipe clean with ease are also available now. See the Product Guide for more information.

Remove racks and clean, with **dish soap,** and then **Bar Keeper's Friend**® for stuck on stains. Wipe down the inside and the glass (**Bar Keeper's Friend** will take burned-on food off of the glass without scratching too!), then rinse clean with a microfiber cloth. Use glass cleaner to bring it to a shine when finished. After the toaster oven is cleaned to satisfaction, replace the drip tray and wipe down the top, front, and sides.

As with most things in the home, cleaning up a mess when it happens is the best practice. Food will harden with each use of the microwave or toaster oven if left to sit on the surface. To make a thorough cleaning as painless as possible, take the time to clean up spills at the time they occur. You'll be glad you made the effort.

Stove Overhead Exhaust

If the stove has an overhead exhaust, remove any filters that can be taken out and soak them in hot water with **dish soap**. If there is a lot of grease on the filters, use **undiluted dish soap** and swirl it around with a light scrubbing. Let them sit for ten minutes or more and then rinse with hot tap water. Air dry and replace.

Clean the underside of the overhead exhaust with **undiluted dish soap** on a damp microfiber cloth to remove grease. If some grease remains stuck on, use **Bar Keeper's Friend**® to remove the tough spots, and wipe clean with a damp cloth. Repeat the same with the outside of the overhead and wipe clean with a damp cloth. If the overhead is stainless steel, once it is clean and dry, use a dry microfiber cloth and **Liquid Gold**® to bring it to a shine.

Stove

If the stove has round, cast iron burner caps, remove those, and remove any cooked on messes with a microfiber cloth and hot, soapy water. Anything that does not come off with that solution will likely come off with a dab of **Bar Keeper's Friend**®.

Continue with the stove top. Dab a quarter-sized spot of **undiluted dish soap** on the stove top. Use a damp microfiber cloth to move the dish soap around the stove top to clean the surface. Most grease and food will come off this way. Other stains may be scrubbed away with a microfiber cloth and **Bar Keeper's Friend**®. Repeat these steps until as much of the mess as possible is removed by the products mentioned. Rinse the cloth and wipe down until it shines. Use **glass cleaner** to give it a shine if needed, unless it is stainless steel.

Return to the sink and check out the gas stove grates or electric stove burner trays and use a cloth to wipe them down. If there is burned on food, **Bar Keeper's Friend**® will take off much, if not all, of it. Test a spot to be sure it doesn't scratch the surface (it shouldn't at all, but better to be safe than sorry) and use a cloth to scrub. If the stove has cast iron gas burner grates, this is where the

stainless steel scrubber can come in handy. Use **Bar Keeper's Friend** on the scrubber and test a small spot to be sure the scrubber doesn't scratch the surface. If it is safe, continue to take off burned-on food that will not come off with the previous methods.

Rinse, air dry, and return to the stove. Electric stove burner trays may be rinsed and dried and replaced under burners.

Ceramic and glass-top stoves may be cleaned in the same way. First, wipe down with **dish soap**. Then, for whatever does not come off, use a microfiber cloth and **Bar Keeper's Friend**® to remove the remaining stains. **Bar Keeper's Friend** should not scratch these surfaces. But, as always, test a small area before tackling the whole surface.

If the knobs are removable, remove them and place them in the sink water and let them soak. Be sure to clean the area under where the knobs sit, as grease builds up and hardens there. **Undiluted dish soap** works well for this area. Wash down the front of the stove with a damp microfiber cloth. If it is a stainless steel stove, wipe it dry, then use **Liquid Gold**® on a dry microfiber cloth and buff in a circular motion to polish. This should wipe away existing, and discourage future, finger prints on the surface.

Oven

Many newer ovens are self-cleaning. When working with a self-cleaning oven, determine if you're comfortable using this feature, follow the instructions to set the oven to clean. Be sure to be present in the home at all times when the oven is on. Oven temperatures in self-cleaning cycles reach over 500 degrees. Once the cycle ends and the oven cools, wipe down the inside, racks, and door glass with a clean, wet cloth. If there are remaining burned on stains, **Bar Keeper's Friend**® will likely take them off.

When working with an oven that is not self-cleaning, use **full strength dish soap** and rub it in. Let set for a minute, then scrub with a damp microfiber cloth. If there are burned on stains that will not come off with the dish soap application, use **Bar Keeper's Friend**® to clean burned messes off of racks and door glass without scratching with a **non-scratch cloth or sponge** as recommended in the Cleaning Tools list. This is a good alternative to toxic oven cleaners.

Once the oven is scrubbed clean to your satisfaction, wipe all inside parts clean with a rinsed microfiber cloth.

Refrigerator

The refrigerator may be a project unto itself, depending upon how frequently it has been cleaned. I'll assume it's pretty dirty and give detailed instruction on how I get it done when it's in this condition. If the refrigerator is fairly clean and it just requires a light cleaning, a simple wipe-down of the inside shelves and outside door surfaces with **Homemade Cleaner** may be sufficient. The best rule of thumb is to clean up messes as they occur. If chocolate syrup or a package of meat leaks all over the top shelf, it should be cleaned up when it happens. The longer it's there, the harder it is to clean. Generally, other than a few crumbs here and there, one can get away with a light cleaning of the door and handle most times and a more thorough cleaning as described below once every six months, depending upon level of use. For a more thorough cleaning, follow the instructions below.

Refrigerator cleaning is best done from the top down. If the freezer needs to be defrosted, get this started when you begin cleaning the kitchen so it can be nearly thawed, or the ice may be more easily removed, by the time you get to it. Turn your refrigerator off using the temperature dial inside, or by unplugging it, and leave the freezer door propped open while you clean the rest of the kitchen. Freezers that collect ice are not working efficiently and need to be repaired or replaced. The most common causes of ice build-up are keeping the freezer open too much, a bad door gasket allowing warm air in, or a leak.

If there is no ice buildup, remove items from the freezer and let the door sit open for about 10 minutes. If the freezer temperature can be turned up so it's not so cold, this will help to keep the surface from freezing up and snagging the cloth or sponge. If the surface is very cold, even a hot soapy cloth will stick to it and make it difficult to clean. Once the surface warms up and can be wiped down easily, apply a light spray of **bleach cleaner** or **Homemade Cleaner,** depending upon the level of cleanliness, to your cloth and wipe down the inside and any racks. If your freezer is a side-by-side, remove the racks and clean them as described in the refrigerator instructions below. If there are marks and scratches inside, these may come off with **Bar Keeper's Friend**®. Give it a final wipe-down with a rinsed cloth and place the food items back in the freezer. Be sure to turn the temperature gauge back to where it originally was. On to the refrigerator!

Remove items from the top shelf and any drawers that may be attached to it. Do one shelf at a time. Notice any foodstuff that should be thrown away. This is a great opportunity to get rid of those three year old jellies and that stir fry from your favorite Hibachi place that have been in the back growing green hair. If it hasn't been used in six months, throw it out, (unless it's an unopened bottle of wine).

If the shelves are removable, take them out one at a time from top to bottom. Make note of what level they are at in the refrigerator to avoid frustration of not fitting back in correctly. The shelf may be a piece of glass that can be lifted out without the frame. If so, carefully remove the glass first, then the frame. Take it over to the sink and wash it in the dishwater. Rinse and lay flat on a dry towel on the counter. Setting it down lowers the risk of dropping it with wet hands and breaking it. These shelves may seem durable when shoving things around on them in the fridge, but not so much when they get dropped on the floor.

While the shelf is out, wipe down the inside top and sides in the area where that shelf resides. Once finished, replace the shelf and/or drawers and replace the food items. Repeat for each shelf. Remove drawers as you go and wash and dry them as with the shelving. Wire shelving is less difficult to wash and not as fragile. These can easily be wiped down in the sink.

Once the inside is finished, repeat the process with the inside door area. Remove items and shelves one at a time, from top to bottom, and note what notches removable shelves belong in for easy replacement. Wash them with a microfiber cloth and **clean, soapy water**. Tough stains may come out better with **spray bleach cleaner**. Before putting food items back on the door shelving, take a moment to wipe the bottoms of the items before setting them in place.

Mold and mildew can build up in ice and water dispensers, so be sure to clean them out well. Use **spray bleach cleaner** to wipe out the dispenser outlets. Bend over and look up into them to get a good look. Wipe down the outside of the refrigerator with a damp cloth until it's clean. If the fridge is stainless steel, give it a nice polish with a dry microfiber cloth and **Liquid Gold®**. It will bring it to a lovely shine and deter fingerprints. Onward!

When finished with dispensers, wipe the door gaskets clean (the rubber seal around the door). This may be black with mildew. **Bar Keeper's Friend** may scrub this away. If it still needs work, rinse the **Bar Keeper's Friend** and then try **spray bleach cleaner.**

When you are satisfied the refrigerator can't get any cleaner, it is finished.

Counter Top

There are many varieties of counter top surfaces. Most of them can be cleaned simply with a clean microfiber cloth and warm, soapy water. If more effort is required, try **Homemade Cleaner** by spraying a bit on stains and letting sit for 10-20 seconds, then wipe clean. White or light colored counter tops can sometimes get cleaner by using **spray bleach cleaner.** Be careful when using bleach cleaners, as they may remove the color from clothing and other fabrics.

If the counters are made of soap stone, no products but warm water should be used on them. To shine, apply lemon oil and let sit overnight. The next day, use a clean, dry microfiber cloth to buff oil away until it shines. For regular cleaning, do not use any sponges or other items that will scrub or scratch the shine away. Simply clean messes up when they occur and use warm water and a microfiber cloth to wipe clean.

Cabinets and Back Splashes

Wipe down cabinet fronts and interiors with a damp cloth and **clean, soapy water**. For real wood cabinets, a final application of **Liquid Gold®**

using a dry microfiber cloth should make them look terrific. Application of **Liquid Gold®** doesn't need to be done at every cleaning, only as needed.

Back splashes may be wiped down with **soapy water** and a clean cloth. If the back splash is a white or light colored surface, stains may be removed more easily using **bleach spray cleaner**, if the back splash is a surface that is deemed safe by the product manufacturer's label.

Sink and Fixtures

Once cleaning of all other areas of the kitchen is complete, finish up by cleaning the sink and fixtures. If the sink and fixtures are light colored, stained, and scratched, great results can be achieved using **Bar Keeper's Friend®** and a **non-scratch Scotch Brite® sponge** to remove those scratches. Once scratches have been removed and the sink has been scrubbed for other blemishes, rinse clean and apply a light coat of **bleach spray cleaner.** Let sit for 5 minutes and rinse clean.

If the sink is dark colored Enamel, a dab of **undiluted dish soap** should clean it well. If there are water stains, use **Scrub Free®** bathroom cleaner to clean the sink and the fixtures. Finish by wiping up all of the water and mess from the surrounding sink area and fixtures with a clean cloth.

A stainless steel sink may have rust, food stains, or just stuck on grime. **Bar Keeper's Friend®** is made for this job. Sprinkle a bit on and get scrubbing with a **non-scratch Scotch Brite® sponge** to bring it to a shine. Rinse when finished. If rust stains are stubborn, use a coat of **Lime Away® spray cleaner** to get them out, then rinse clean.

I cannot say this enough…clean up water and food messes as they happen. Water seems harmless enough. But in reality, it can do a lot of damage to your surfaces and fixtures if left to sit without wiping it up. Lime, rust, and corrosion all occur with standing water. To make cleaning easier, be sure to keep standing water wiped up.

Odds and Ends

Any kitchen may have miscellaneous items that will need to be cleaned that I may not have addressed here. If there is wood furniture that has years of dirt and grease on it, wipe it down with warm, **soapy water** and a clean cloth. This can be used for wiping down pan racks, furniture, walls, baseboards, you name it…look around the room and find what's dirty and clean it. Is the garbage can filthy? Empty it and wash it down, inside and out, let it dry and put a clean bag in it. Are the insides of cupboards and drawers dirty? Vacuum out and wipe down with a damp cloth.

As I move around the kitchen to wipe down counter tops, shelves, furniture, etc, I lift items that are in the way and wipe under them, replace them and move on. If there is clutter, so what? Pick it up another day and be sure to clean under and around it so when you do remove it, the area looks clean. The exception to this is bookshelves that have a lot of books or knick knacks. For a thorough cleaning, one can lift these items up and clean under them. For regular cleaning on a weekly or bi-weekly basis, clean these areas with a feather duster. Why would you need to dust under something when no dust can get under there? This is only good for so long, mind you. After a while, a good cleaning is in order and items should be picked up and full shelves should be cleaned. Every other month, perhaps?

Floors all through the house will be completed last, so don't worry about dropping crumbs and wiping the dust and dirt onto the floor. Use good judgment though. Don't wipe a blob of jelly onto the floor because that would just be disgusting. But, if when cleaning out the toaster oven or anything else, crumbs get on the floor, don't worry about it. They will be picked up by the vacuum when the higher cleaning tasks have been completed.

I've given you the down and dirty instructions for how I get the toughest surfaces in the kitchen clean. It's up to you to know your personal kitchen space, to find the messes and to get them and keep them clean using these products and instructions. To move around the kitchen most efficiently from task to task, follow the order below.

Kitchen Order:

1. Dishwasher- Get this job started so the dishwasher is running while other tasks are being completed.
2. Refrigerator- This can be the biggest job. Make a mess cleaning it out so that cleanup can be included when cleaning the rest of the kitchen.
3. Microwave- If this is over the stove, clean it before cleaning the stove so crumbs and drips don't get on the nice clean stove. If it's on the counter, wipe it out before cleaning the counters. Be sure to lift the microwave and clean under it, if you are able.
4. Overhead exhaust- Clean this before the stove to keep from dropping things on the clean stove top.
5. Stove/oven- Clean this before the counter tops, so counters can be used to place drying grates and stove top parts to dry.
6. Counter-top appliances

7. Cupboards- Front (and inside if time allows), shelves and back splash
8. Miscellaneous areas and furniture
9. Sink and fixtures- Save this until nearly finished, as water will be needed right up to the bitter end.
10. Counter tops- Give the counter tops one final wipe down before calling it done.
11. Floors

Once the kitchen is cleaned to satisfaction, take a look around once more to be sure everything that can be seen is clean. If it isn't, use a damp cloth and do a quick and final once-over. Now…stand back and smile.

Moving on!

CLUTTER

In order to move on and get to the next task in the cleaning order, the issue of clutter must be addressed. Clutter is the bane of our existence. Unless you are obsessive/compulsive about neatness, your clutter invades all areas of your home. Either your underwear are on the floor or clothing is draped on a chair. There may be stacks of magazines you'll never read, bills and mail on the counter, knick-knacks you can't remember buying and never look at. You name it, it's in your house and it's clutter.

It's time to take a hard look at all of it and weed it out. Find a large Rubbermaid storage tote and start looking at your things. Have you worn that sweater in two years? "No", you say? Heave it in the tote. Can you sit down right now, today, and peruse those magazines to find whatever articles you might want to read in-depth soon and throw out any that don't contain such articles? If you can, sit down, page through them all. If there is an article you want to read in full, tear it out and then throw the magazine in the recycling bin.

Do this with every magazine and then promise this week, after you've tucked yourself into bed at night, you will keep a light on and read these articles until you can put all of your torn out pages in the recycle bin at the end of the week. If you can't commit to this much, toss them without looking through them. Make note of the magazines you recycled without reading. Don't renew them.

If you have mail, sort the junk from the necessary. Then throw out the junk. Open all mail you deemed necessary and re-assess once it's opened if it is still necessary. Keep what is, throw out what isn't. From this point on, tend to your mail the day you get it. This alleviates piles of clutter that collect over time and seem difficult to overcome.

Is that coconut gorilla you got at the petting zoo on your trip to Florida as a seven year old growing spider webs? Do you ever even look at it? If not, take a picture of it, then throw it out. Do this with every knick-knack you don't actually pick up from time to time and get a smile on your face from the feeling it gives you. Everything that lays around your house with no purpose, even if that purpose is to make you notice it and smile because of it, is just collecting dust and making your home messier and harder to clean.

As I was growing up, several events occurred that resulted in me losing many of my personal belongings and sentimental treasures. Because of this, I really understand the connections we feel to these odds and ends that come into our lives. I have always saved my children's treasures and artwork and worthy projects because I have an attachment to them, they don't. Or, at least they think they don't. The only attachment I have to them is that when each of them is settled in their own home (they are all over 21 now), I will bring their belongings over with a bottle of wine and we will go through them all and laugh and smile. I will leave that day knowing I have done my part. And I will leave those things with them. They can throw them away, burn them, save them, I don't care. All I know is that when I get home, I will have more closet space for myself!

It can be difficult to give things up for sure. But, through experience, I have learned that we can overcome these feelings and even be liberated by the practice of de-cluttering our homes and our lives. For instance, about eight years ago, we remodeled our home. Nearly every single room was torn up and redone. This project was organized right down to the nuts and bolts by me. But, I also knew that in order to complete it, I had to be willing to unload a lot of things to make our new spaces look fresh and comfortable. The rule I set for myself was that in every room I had to get rid of HALF of everything. HALF. Not just a few things, not an unused item here or there, but HALF of EVERYTHING in our home.

Look around your home. In just the room you are sitting in, try to imagine half of the items in your room that you would be willing to part with. Not easy is it? Well, I can say with great pride that I met this goal and I have only regretted it twice, only for about a day each time, and then it was forgotten. I can recall only twice that I wondered where an item was that I really wish I had and this didn't even happen until a couple of years later, so I couldn't have missed these things too much. We develop bad habits like saving a broken door knob because some year we might need a screw from that door knob and we'll know right where we can find one…if only we save that door knob now and squirrel it away in some drawer or closet. Don't let your mind convince you to do these silly things. Break free from the clutter!

You don't have to start with a goal as radical as mine was. I only went as far as 50% of my stuff because I didn't have anywhere to put it all when the house was being torn apart. I couldn't just stash it all in another room when every room was being demolished, could I?

Take another look and determine a good number to start with. How about ten? Can you go into every room and find ten things you are willing to part with? Sure you can. Now, go to it! If it makes you feel better about parting with your belongings, put them in a bin for a local goodwill organization. Post an ad on Craigslist or Freecycle and tell someone who needs it more than you to come and get it for free. Once you've removed ten items from each room, you can stand back and be proud of yourself! Then, come back and do the same thing next month and every month after. Don't worry, you won't shrink the amount of your belongings to nothing by doing this. We are constantly dragging new and useless stuff into our homes on a weekly basis. You will not be deprived. Trust me.

Decluttering is a habit we all need to get better at. Many of us are already minimalists. This is admirable, but a little overboard for me. I like stuff. I like to have stuff around me to make me feel cozy. But stuff better not get in my way or I might just lose it. There is a happy medium to be found. Find yours and then feel good about it. Once you empty your bins either by donating, recycling, or throwing away, find a nice spot in the corner of a bedroom or closet where you can keep a bin. You will be surprised at how nice it is to have it there to place things in as you go through your days and weeks. I find that I will now open a cupboard to get a glass and see a bread dish or coffee mugs that I haven't used in years. A wave comes over me and I pick up the item and take it to the next room and place it in the bin. It will hopefully find a purpose and have a happy use for someone else in the world, and that makes me smile.

Solutions for Clutter

1. Set a goal for how much you will commit to de-cluttering your home
2. Find three receptacles for cleaning out: Donate, Trash, Recycle
3. Weed out old mail, magazines, and other non-essential paper
4. Reassess your keepsakes. If you can let go of it, take a photo of it to remember it by, and let it go.
5. Pass on treasures to others who might enjoy them.
6. Repeat 1-5 often.

Now that we've eliminated the clutter and will continue to do so as time goes on, we can see our surfaces in order to dust them and keep them clean. Onward!

LIVING AREAS

In twenty years, I have dusted for over 10,000 hours. Just calculating this makes me feel ill. Dusting is my least favorite task in all of house cleaning. Give me five bathrooms to clean and I would prefer it over dusting the house any day. It's tedious, tiresome, dirty, just like raking. And I don't like raking either. In fact, we build our own furniture, and almost always leave our finishes flat or light colored in order to avoid seeing any dust on the surface. Yes, that is how thoroughly thoughtful I am about avoiding dusting in my own home.

I used to use furniture polish, and sometimes, I might still. But for the most part, I use a clean, lightly dampened microfiber cloth. If things are pretty dusty, the cloth may need rinsing several times over the course of the work, making sure to wring it out well so standing water isn't left on the furniture. A feather duster is also a great tool for quick dusting or dusting items that are more fragile and shouldn't be picked up often.

To dust, wipe down as many parts of the item you're cleaning as possible. Clean under any piece from time to time as well. Be sure to remove or lift items in the area that's being cleaned. Rinse and wring out the microfiber cloth regularly, making sure to wring as much water as possible to keep from leaving standing water on surfaces.

Move around the perimeter of each room and dust furniture, lamps, bookshelves, baseboards and picture frames (on and off of the wall). After the perimeter of the room is finished, head for the center and wipe down any items, including microfiber sofas and chairs (they look nice when a microfiber cloth is used to brush crumbs off), leather chairs, ottomans, coffee tables, etc. With experience, this becomes a much more fluid activity that takes less time.

Electronics can be tricky to work around. Comfort level in spaces with electronic equipment may vary. If you are uncomfortable getting too far into the tangles of cords, give it a quick feather dusting. If you aren't intimidated, dive in and lift things up and clean under them, being careful not to disconnect anything.

A feather duster is a good tool for quick touch-ups, as long as it removes the dust. Feather dust knick-knacks and books, as well as baseboards and tops of window frames to remove cobwebs. If you have children or pets, look at the walls and door frames at knee height for dirt, grime, food, spit and snot marks. These areas can get very dirty when we share our homes with children (and pets). For more thorough cleanings, a lightly damp micro-fiber cloth is recommended.

If the microfiber cloth gets really dirty, rinse it out in the sink and wring it out very well, or get a fresh, clean cloth. No leaky, dripping water should be coming off of your cloth.

We don't often think about dusting our walls, but if it's never been done, it probably should be. Gently use the vacuum with a hard floor attachment for walls. For areas that gather a lot of dust such as bookshelves, behind beds and other furniture, ceiling fans, window casings, and inside furniture cushions, use the hose without attachments. Door jams (the frames around doors) and light switches may be wiped down to remove cobwebs and fingerprints.

If there are washable curtains in the room (check for a label), look them over. Are they dirty? If there is a lot of dust in the room, the tops will likely be dirty. If there are animals in the home and the curtains reach the floor, they will likely be dirty toward the bottom. If they are, and they can be washed, take them down and wash them. This will make the room look and smell much better and it's a relatively simple task…the washer does all the work. Allow curtains to air dry for best results, or follow the directions on the label. Curtains often shrink or get very wrinkled when dried in the dryer. If they need a light iron once dried, do so with the iron set on a low temp to protect the fabric. Hang them up and enjoy them in a nice, clean room.

If there are pieces of furniture that would look nice polished after cleaning the dust off, I use **Liquid Gold**®. Spray on a dry microfiber cloth, not on the furniture. Remove items from the furniture and use the cloth to buff in a circular motion until it shines.

Once the dusting is finished in each room, take a quick glance upward. Are there cobwebs? The vacuum may be used to clean cobwebs. If the room has higher ceilings than the vacuum will reach, a cobweb brush with a telescoping pole would be a solid investment. This task shouldn't need to be done more than once per month, unless the home has wood or forced air heat during the cold months. During these times, more dust collects in higher spaces so it might need to be done more often. When in doubt, look up.

Dusting isn't hard. It requires a good eye and the intention to be thorough at least once every month. Outside of that, a light feather dusting or quick wipe down of the most visible or high-traffic areas where most time is spent should be sufficient. Focus on what can be seen and what makes the room most comfortable to be in rather than a strict regimen. But don't let it go too long or a thorough cleaning will be in order again, and none of us has time for that.

A Dust Free Routine

1. Use a lightly damp cloth to leave no standing water on furniture. Rinse and wring out frequently
2. Dust from top to bottom; windows, walls, furniture and surfaces, items on surfaces, inside furniture, baseboards and molding
3. Check curtains and window treatment for cleaning needs

4. From time to time, polish nice wood pieces with **Liquid Gold**®, or other favorite furniture polish

Does the living area look finished?

Test #1: Sit in your favorite spot in each room, the place where you spend the most time. Now, look around you in a close circle, about two feet out from you. Do you see anything that should be cleaned? If not, widen your circle another six feet. Anything that still needs cleaning? Now, look up and all around you. How's it look? Are you satisfied?

Test #2: Do you have company coming? Sit where they will sit when they visit. Repeat Test #1. How's it look? Are you satisfied?

If you said "yes", congratulations!! You'll be an expert in no time!

BEDROOM

The bedroom is a sacred space. Since my husband and I built our beautiful bed (a light-colored and low dust surface) and invested in a thirteen inch thick memory foam mattress, I cannot count the number of times I've snuggled into my bed, heaved a sigh of relief and said, "I love my bed." Having a clean and lovely space to settle into at the end of whatever your day looks like is an important gift to give to yourself. Whether you sleep on a hand crafted bed, a futon, or an air mattress on the floor, take care to create a comfortable space to serve as your sanctuary for rest.

The obvious place to start is with the bed. Wash bed sheets no less than once every other week. Other bedding, like washable blankets, quilts, and comforters, can be washed every 3 months minimum unless they seem to need cleaning more frequently. Having a second set of sheets offers the freedom to wash the other set when it's convenient. Remove sheets and pillowcases and wash and dry them. Using fabric softener and medium to low dryer temps may cut down on wrinkling.

Folding clean sheets can be a challenge. Many clients ask me to teach them how to fold sheets and they are so proud once they get the hang of it! It's mind-boggling how confusing this simple task can seem, so I understand the urge to just wad them up in a bundle in frustration. However, pulling neatly folded sheets out of the linen closet to put on the bed is a treat. Otherwise, it feels like putting wadded up, dirty sheets back on the bed. What's the point in that? The idea is to feel like your home is clean and comfortable. There are many videos and tutorials on the Internet that explain how to correctly fold sheets. Find a source you like and learn from it.

Bed Making

There are many ways to make a bed. If you have a modest home with simple bedding, don't you still want it to be inviting when you walk into your bedroom to let go of the day behind you? A made bed is a healthy way to start your good night's sleep. There are videos available on how to make a bed that you can research for yourself if you need that level of instruction. The Internet is also full of images of fancy ways to make up the bed that you can copy if you're really serious about it. For our purposes, I will simply assume that you know how to complete this task and will determine for yourself the level of sophistication with which you present this centerpiece of your lovely, clean bedroom.

Bedroom Dusting

Keep bedroom furniture free of dust. You spend a lot of time sleeping there, so clutter and books, paper and knick-knacks around your bed are best kept at a minimum, especially if you have allergies. Be sure to wipe down all furniture with a lightly dampened microfiber cloth to remove dust. For thorough dusting, pick up items and clutter and dust under them. For quicker, lighter cleanings, you can work around your light clutter and piles of magazines, mail, etc. in order to keep things tidy in between thorough cleanings.

Dust collects in a few places that are not so obvious and can wreak havoc on an allergic person. On the wall and floor behind the bed, as well as the bottom edge of the headboard are all places we don't often think to look. Baseboards also collect a lot of dust. Be sure to tend to these spaces from time to time. It may not be necessary to get to them every time you clean, but once a month would be a good schedule. It's as simple as running a vacuum hose or a feather duster over the area, so it should not take that much more time.

Closets are full of dust. If you hoard clothing, closets fill up fast with items that go untouched. When you have a chance, take the time to pull everything out of the closet and remove anything you have not worn in a year or more. The only exceptions are family heirlooms and three special pieces of clothing you can't bear to let go of. If you stick to these two simple categories, the possibility of missing something once it's gone is nearly non-existent.

The floor under your bed is a good place for neat storage. Use rolling plastic bins or giant zippered storage bags to utilize this hidden space efficiently while keeping the items you store free from dust bunnies that collect under your bed in between cleanings. Be sure to pull things out from time to time to dust and vacuum the space. A vacuum can also help maximize space by using vacuum seal, space-saving bags to store your fabric belongings.

Bedroom Routine

7. Create and maintain an inviting sleeping space. Wash bedding regularly.
8. Dust surfaces and tidy to maintain a comfortable, relaxing environment.
9. Give attention to closets and spaces behind furniture monthly to keep dust from collecting.
10. Utilize spaces under furniture for storing items that are used infrequently. Store in containers that can easily be moved for cleaning.

Look up, look down, look all around. Like what you see? Let's move on.

BATHROOM

The bathroom is as difficult to keep clean as the kitchen and just as important. Keeping a clean bathroom cuts down on illness and provides you with a safe and sanitary space to do your business and get ready for your day. There are so many different styles and materials used in bathrooms that it has taken some doing to find solutions to bathroom cleaning challenges that will work on most of these surfaces without needing a box full of products.

Begin by filling a bucket about a third of the way full with hot water. Add a dollop (instructions on the label) of the **disinfectant all-purpose cleaner** mentioned in the Cleaning Products section of this book. A **microfiber cloth** and a **non-scratch** scrubbing sponge will round out the tools for the following tasks.

Showers and Tubs

Let's start with the shower. For glass shower doors, step into the shower and spray down one door with **Scrub Free® Bathroom Cleaner**, the bathroom cleaner mentioned in the Cleaning Products section of this book. Let it sit for thirty seconds and then begin rubbing in a circular motion with the microfiber cloth. You should begin to see a difference in the way the shower door looks. Once the door has been fully scrubbed with the cloth, rinse and wring out the cloth. Wipe the door clean from top to bottom, rinsing and wringing out your cloth as needed. A second application may be needed. **Scrub Free® Bathroom Cleaner** works really well, but if the shower hasn't been cleaned and the soap scum and water stains have been allowed to collect on shower doors for a long time, more than one application may be necessary.

For really tough water stain, I have had success applying **Lime-Away® spray cleaner** mentioned in the **Cleaning Products** section to glass doors and letting it sit for about 30 seconds. *(Be completely sure that all of the previous Scrub Free® product has been rinsed from the area before applying another product!)* Repeat this section by section until satisfied with the way it looks. This cleaner removes almost all water stains when given a chance to work its magic. Then, wipe it clean, making sure to rinse and wring out the cloth as needed. Repeat this process with the other door.

Shower door tracks can be a difficult to maintain. These often have stuck-on water stains and lime deposits. I have also had success with cleaning door tracks with the **Lime-Away® spray cleaner**. Whichever cleaner is used, apply it and then let it sit. Use the edge of a sponge or a toothbrush to scrub the crud off of the track and then pour water into it to rinse. Be sure if a different cleaner was used on it first, that it is completely rinsed before introducing another cleaner. **NEVER mix chemical cleaning products.**

For shower doors that are not horribly stained and don't need extra scrubbing, a simple cleaning with **Scrub Free® Bathroom Cleaner** should suffice. Once they are cleaned and rinsed, let them dry, inside and out, and then apply glass cleaner and wipe down with a paper towel or dry microfiber cloth for a streak-free shine.

Shower curtains and rubber bath mats may be washed in the washing machine on medium temperature with a quarter cup of white vinegar to remove stains, water deposits, and odors. For mold and mildew stains, use 1/4 cup of bleach in the washing machine instead of vinegar for bleach-safe items.

Shower Walls

Shower walls come in many different textures. Porcelain, ceramic, glass, marble or granite tile, acrylic, ceramic, and painted metal are some of the surfaces you will find in homes today. Word of advice: if you are going to tile your shower, do not use white grout. It is a terrible design mistake. Removing mildew and mold stains from white grout successfully is extremely difficult and almost never brings about satisfying results. In the end, you spend a lot of money and have something that simply cannot stay clean by design and circumstance. It cannot be sealed well enough to inhibit mold and mildew growth over time.

The bathroom is a humid room and white or light grout is a surface that mildew is highly visible on. It's a lose-lose situation. Do not listen to any advice you hear about how bleach cleaner will remove mold and mildew from white grout. After twenty years, I have never found a product that will return this type of surface to it's clean, original state once it has been left to stain, no matter what all those "as seen on TV" products tell you.

For nearly every shower wall surface, **Scrub Free® Bathroom Cleaner** will work. This product will do the same great job of removing water stains, soap scum and dirt on every surface. If the shower and tub aren't too dirty, this product will help get it cleaner more easily with less scrubbing. If there is a tough job ahead, more than one scrubbing sponge and a microfiber cloth and a couple of applications of **Scrub Free®** may be necessary. For those who don't have a large mess, the following instructions may seem like overkill. If so, just use the method I describe once and if that's enough to get the job done, go out to the kitchen and make yourself a cup of tea and sit down for a bit. You've been working hard!

To begin, spray down one wall with **Scrub Free®** so it coats as much area as possible. Let sit for 30 seconds, then begin at the top with either a **microfiber cloth** for easier messes or a **scratch-free scrubbing sponge** for much tougher jobs. Begin rubbing in a circular motion and work until you get as close to a smooth and clean surface as free of water stains and soap scum as possible. Rinse and wring out the cloth or sponge as needed and, beginning at the top of the wall, wipe the soapy mess clean. It may be necessary to rinse it with water after this. If so, use a large plastic cup filled with water, or a removable shower sprayer, and rinse the wall until all of the cleaner is removed. Rinsing may give you a better idea of how much more you will need to work, if any, to get it really clean. If it looks significantly better but still has water stain and soap scum on the wall, another application, now that one layer has been removed, may make it sparkle. Repeat the previous instructions until satisfied that it will not come any cleaner.

The same process can be used for the bottom of your tub, whether it is a flat acrylic surface, or a skid-free surface with tiny squares that dirt and soap scum get stuck in. For non-skid surfaces, a scrub brush might come in handy, scrubbing in a circular motion for most effective cleaning to get stuck-in stains out. The bottom six inches of the tub and where it meets the floor collect the most scum. Pay particular attention to this area. It may need multiple applications. Once all of the tub or shower floor has been scrubbed, rinse as described previously, so you can get a good look at what more can be done. If you are not satisfied or are confident more can be removed, reapply as many times as it takes to be happy with it.

If the shower walls are tile with white grout and there are mildew stains in between some or many tiles, be sure the **Scrub Free® Bathroom Cleaner** is completely rinsed and apply **bleach spray cleaner** to the areas that have mildew stains. Let it sit for a few minutes and then use an old toothbrush to scrub these areas as clean as you can get them. Once again, multiple applications may be needed. Once rinsed, if the bleach cleaner does not give the desired result, an application of **Bar Keeper's Friend**® with a toothbrush may help.

If there is caulk around the bottom edge of the shower walls that has black mildew stains that will not come out, peel off the caulk and purchase a new tube of caulk and reapply neatly. There are video instructions on the Internet that detail how to apply caulk properly. It will be less frustrating and give more satisfying results than time wasted trying to get the old caulk clean. It will never happen.

Once an initial deep cleaning of the shower walls has been done and it is as clean as it will get, routine cleaning will consist of spraying on the cleaner, and wiping down the walls with a microfiber cloth until they are smooth and free of soap scum and water stains. Then, either wipe them down with a rinsed cloth, a large plastic cup with water, or shower sprayer. If this task is done every one or two weeks, it should be a breeze to complete.

If the tub is porcelain or painted metal, and it is difficult to get it clean with just this process, **Bar Keeper's Friend**® will help get rust stains and scratches off the surface of the tub. Once the tub looks great, rinse thoroughly and step back and admire your work!

Toilets

Lime-Away® **toilet bowl cleaner** does a remarkable job on toilets. Squirt the product all around the inside of the toilet bowl and let it sit for a few minutes. The worse the toilet looks, the longer is should sit. Five minutes ought to be long enough for most stains. If it isn't, you can reapply. Use a **ScotchBrite® sponge** for this part of the bathroom cleaning.

While waiting, use the bucket of water with **all-purpose disinfectant cleaner like Lysol®** to rinse the sponge and wipe around the outside of the toilet bowl and the bottom where it bolts into the floor. This is a particularly dirty area, especially if there are males in the home. Be sure to look at the underside of the toilet to wipe clean. This area doesn't get too dirty regularly, but after a while, mildew and cobwebs may build up if it rarely gets attention. Be sure to clean the floor around the base of the toilet. This area generally needs more attention than just the vacuuming and mopping that will get done later.

The underside of the toilet seat does get stained often. You may have success with **Bar Keeper's Friend**® in this area if stains are stubborn. The toilet bowl lid and the area where the seat bolts onto the toilet should be cleaned carefully. The bolted areas often have caps that open up for easier cleaning. Take the opportunity once in a while to do this and to get them cleaned out for best results.

Once finished with the outside of the toilet, begin scrubbing the inside of the bowl. **Lime-Away**® **toilet bowl cleaner** should remove most, if not all, of the grime from the bowl. Scrub with the **scratch-free sponge** until no more will come off. Flush the toilet. If satisfied, the job is done. If there are still stains, reapply **Lime-Away**® **toilet bowl cleaner** and let it sit for another couple of minutes before scrubbing again. Flush once again. If there are still stains, **Bar Keeper's Friend**® may help. Try an application of **Bar Keeper's Friend**® on the scrubbing side of the sponge and scrub the stain. If it comes off, yay! If not, it's there for life. Flush and be happy it doesn't look like it did when you began.

Sinks and Vanities

This is a simple task. Follow the same instructions for the tub basin and that should work for most surfaces. **Scrub Free**® **Bathroom Cleaner** should remove built-up soap scum and water stains. If the sink is painted cast iron or porcelain, **Bar Keeper's Friend**® can remove scuffs and rust stains.

Wipe down the vanity top with **Scrub Free**® to remove water spots and soap build-up. Rinse with a damp cloth that is wrung out well to avoid leaving standing water on the surface. If the sink is made of a specialty surface like metal, follow the advice of the manufacturer for proper cleaning.

Fixtures

Even in areas where the water is terrific, you will experience water stain and lime build-up. Water does a lot of damage in areas where there is repeated use. If you don't stay on top of it, lime deposits and rust will eat away at your fixtures. The best way to avoid this is to keep them cleaned regularly.

I have had success with **Lime-Away® spray cleaner** for really tough jobs around the edges of fixtures where they meet the sink, and there is usually a good build-up of rust and water stain. This may be safe to use on fixtures without damaging the finish. Read the label to determine if the finish is safe to use this product on.

Mirrors

Be sure to wipe mirrors and the exterior of shower doors clean with a dry cloth or paper towel and glass cleaner for a sparkling bathroom finish.

Bathroom Routine

1. Begin with the tub/shower, starting with doors. Move on to the shower walls, fixtures, and tub basin in that order
2. Clean toilet from top to bottom and inside bowl
3. Clean sink, vanity, and fixtures
4. Check shower curtain cleanliness, moisture stains on walls, wipe mirrors clean

Look around. Does your bathroom look better than it has in years? Hurray for you! On to the floors!

FLOORS

There are so many floor surfaces, but thankfully, only a few techniques for getting them clean. From wood to tile, travertine to slate, laminate, bamboo, clay and carpeting, cleaning the floor is a simple task, but can be physically demanding. For this reason, having the best equipment possible for completing the job is necessary. See the Cleaning Tools section of this book for information on what type of vacuum will best meet the goal of cleaning your home most efficiently and effectively. Once the proper tools are in hand, the floors await!

Vacuuming

Clean the floors last. After all other tasks are completed, and all the dust and crumbs from furniture and counter tops have been brushed onto the floor, then they can be cleaned. This is the end of the line, the final frontier. Once the floors are finished, you can take a step back and look at these sparkling spaces with pride. But alas, we get ahead of ourselves.

The objective is to get your home as clean as you possibly can, and in that pursuit, the vacuum is your friend. Use it for as many tasks as you can. The vacuum is the tool to be used to clean over, under, and in everything.

Move furniture that can be moved easily. And clean the floor underneath. Any furniture that can't be moved easily, but you can reach the vacuum wand under, should be cleaned under. If the furniture has removable cushions, remove them and vacuum inside the furniture.

Take this opportunity to look at walls and ceiling areas, especially in corners where cobwebs and dust collect. The hard-floor attachment works well for these purposes. Be sure to look carefully and catch all the dust you can with the vacuum. It will make mopping much more effective and efficient.

Once the flat, hard surfaces have been cleaned, replace the power-head and clean any area rugs and carpeted spaces. If you have darkened edges on wall-to-wall carpet where dirt has collected, remove the power-head and use the hose/wand to clean the edges. The power-head can also be helpful in removing pet hair from furniture. Some canister vacuums even come with a smaller, suction driven power-head for this purpose.

TIP: Try to avoid walking from rooms that have not been vacuumed to rooms that have already been vacuumed. Dragging dirt and animal hair into clean spaces will cause this dirt and hair to get into your mop once you begin washing the floors. One way to solve this is to vacuum and mop as you go, mopping a room as soon as you've finished vacuuming it and then moving on to other rooms.

Once you've thoroughly cleaned your spaces using the method I've included here, you can get a sense over time how frequently each of these areas needs to be cleaned. It isn't likely that your furniture needs to be vacuumed out each week, but perhaps once a month. Your curtains and walls probably won't collect dust each week either. But a good going over with the vacuum every so often would be a good habit to get into. Each time you vacuum your floors, glance upward to see if the corners of door frames or the ceiling have cobwebs that need to be removed. These collect pretty frequently, so regular maintenance is recommended. You know your spaces better than anyone. If you see an area that looks dirty and a vacuum will do the trick, tend to it and get it clean.

Washing Floors

Once your vacuuming is complete, it's time to wash those floors. While figuring out how to vacuum your floors to remove loose dirt is fairly straight forward, there's a bit more of a challenge to washing them correctly. The first challenge is determining what type of flooring you have and what type of cleaner is safe to use on it.

Prepare a bucket filled with hot water up to about 5 inches from the top. Without adding anything, this can be used to clean just about any hard surface including laminate, stone, tile, hard wood, linoleum, travertine, vinyl, engineered wood, and bamboo. Use the twist mop mentioned in the Cleaning Tools section of this book. Dip the mop in the bucket, then lift it out of the water and twist to wring out excess water over the bucket. Wring out the mop as necessary, so there is not an abundance of standing water left behind when you move it around on the floor.

If you would like to add a little extra cleaning boost and perhaps a pleasant smell to the room, I have had success adding any of the following products to the water bucket:

For laminate, linoleum, travertine, vinyl, and stone floors, add **2 TBSP of Mr. Clean® or Lysol® disinfectant cleaner.** These may be infused with a lemon or citrus scent or other scent that may be pleasing to you.

For wood, engineered wood, or bamboo, add **1/4 cup mixture of equal parts (1/8 cup to 1/8 cup) lemon juice and white vinegar.**

One tablespoon of chemical-free dish soap like Seventh Generation™ or Mrs. Meyer's Clean Day® may be used in place of either solution for all floors. These products have a variety of pleasant scents like Lemon Verbena, Lavender, Geranium, and Basil. Any of these will leave a fresh scent and clean surface.

Begin by dipping your mop in the bucket, then twist to wring it out as well as you can over the bucket. There should be no water dripping from the mop. The mop, when wrung out properly, will not drench your floors with water.

Begin at the end of the room farthest from the door you will exit from. Always mop your way out of a room and do not walk on it again until it's dry. This will avoid footprints and streaks. Move the mop in a swirling motion to reach all areas of the surface. You may need to push on it more firmly to scrub out messes from heavily soiled areas.

Be sure to rinse and wring out your mop frequently as you move through the entire surface of your floor, especially after mopping very dirty areas. If you don't, you'll be dragging dirt around and leaving streaks. Be sure to get into the corners well to remove dirt that has gathered there.

If the floor is tile with grout, the **Goo Gone®** **Grout Cleaner** described in the Cleaning Products section of this book works great on deeply stained floor grout. Spray a little on and let it sit. Scrub out with a scrub brush and it lifts the dirt right out of the grout. This is a product that really does what it claims on floor grout. It does not, in my experience, clean mildew from bathroom grout well, unfortunately.

If your floor is very dirty, you will need to empty the bucket and refill with clean water. You may need to do this several times, depending upon how long it's been since you've given your floors this thorough of a cleaning. Once the water in the bucket is brown, it's a good idea to dump it out and start fresh. For difficult stains on linoleum floors, **Homemade Cleaner** sprayed directly on the floor and left to sit for a minute may bring up ground-in dirt more easily. Either wipe by hand with a micro-fiber cloth or mop clean. Let your floors air dry without walking on them, if possible, to avoid dried-on foot prints.

Once you've finished, move on to other rooms until you've mopped all of your hard floor surfaces. Before putting the mop away, be sure to rinse it in a bucket of clean water and wring it out very well. Be sure there isn't any water dripping from the mop. You may store the mop either by hanging it from a hook or in the empty bucket to air dry.

When you've used your mop five or six times, it is a good idea to wash it in the washing machine.

You can do this by removing the mop head from the handle following the directions provided and placing the mop head in a linen bag. It can be washed in hot water for best results, but any temperature will do. You can add a 1/4 cup of bleach to the wash water for sanitizing, or simply using laundry soap will get it clean. Once it has completed the wash, leave the mop head in the linen bag and place in the dryer for 20 minutes or so. It should be fluffed up and ready to use again. Remove from the linen bag and replace the mop head onto the handle. The mop head will be good for 3 or 4 washings, then may need to be replaced. Note: the mop head must be washed and dried in a linen bag. If not, it will come out in an unusable, tangled mess.

Linen bags can be found in the laundry section of most grocery or discount stores. A small bag, approximately 12″ x 12″ is best to keep the mop head from tangling.

Floor Cleaning Routine

1. Pick up items that are cluttering the floor
2. Vacuum hard floors
3. Wash/mop hard floors
4. Allow to air dry before walking on them
5. Vacuum carpets and area rugs
6. Keep vacuum bag changed regularly and wash mop head to avoid dirt and odors

And then, the floors were done...

EXTRAS

There are a few areas of the home that require special attention from time to time but aren't too difficult to take on. However, it's helpful to have a routine for cleaning them, as well as properly maintaining them. Some of these items are listed below.

Ceiling fans- Be sure the fan is off. Use a damp microfiber cloth to clean the tops and bottoms of the fan blades. Take off any removable light fixtures. These can be washed carefully in warm, soapy water and air dried. Replace the light fixtures when dried.

Windows- Fill a bucket with hot water. Use a damp microfiber cloth and **Homemade Cleaner** to clean grime off of window glass and frames. Wipe clean, rinsing your cloth regularly so you don't smear muck all over the window as you're cleaning it. Be sure to wipe out the window sill and frames. Let dry. Do a final wipe down of the glass with a glass cleaner or with vinegar in a spray bottle and a dry microfiber cloth.

Window Blinds- Window blinds can be frustrating to clean. There are many styles. Some have thin plastic slats, some wood or manufactured wood, cloth, aluminum, and more. There isn't really an easy way to get them clean. You can purchase a specialty **window blind tool** to clean them with, or you can simply use a microfiber cloth. For dusty blinds, use a dry cloth. For dirtier blinds with bug spots or set in dirt and dust, wash clean by filling a bucket with warm water and dish soap, then dampen your cloth and wash each slat.

The frequency with which you need to clean window blinds varies. Cheaper plastic blinds don't need to be cleaned as often, and may simply need a wipe down with a dry cloth while the blinds are closed. Wider plantation style blinds will need cleaning more frequently, at least twice a month, to keep them from collecting thick dust. The frequency also depends upon the type of heat in your home (wood, forced air, etc…) and whether or not you have pets. Wood and forced air heat will push more dust into the air to settle on blinds, requiring more frequent cleaning.

Cloth blinds can be vacuumed for easy cleaning. If something stains cloth blinds, follow your manufacturer's recommendations for cleaning. You may have luck with **Resolve**® laundry stain remover. If you use this product, be sure to try a small, hidden area first to avoid damaging the fabric.

Light Fixtures- Take off removable glass globes from light fixtures that you can reach safely and wash them in warm soapy water. Air dry and replace.

Heating Units- Items in your home that provide heat such as forced air vents, electric baseboard heating units, and radiators can be cleaned to keep dusty odors at a minimum. All can be cleaned with a vacuum using a small brush attachment, and electric baseboard heaters and radiators may collect dust on top of them that can be wiped clean with a damp cloth. Be sure these items are not on and supplying heat at the time you are cleaning them to avoid injury.

Garbage- Change garbage bags frequently to avoid rodents, bugs, and odors. Kitchen and bathroom garbage should be removed from the home, at a minimum, weekly. Garbage that contains food or personal hygiene products may need to be removed more frequently.

Once your home is clean, you will begin to notice the areas that need more attention that have not been mentioned in this book. Each home is unique and has it's own interesting spaces. Adapt the methods mentioned here to best suit each task in order to make your home as clean and inviting as possible.

USING YOUR NEW SKILLS

I hope the methods I've laid out in this book will help you get your home clean now. A thorough cleaning such as I've described need only be done once if you follow the plan on a lighter scale on a regular basis. These methods will make your home very clean and look great.

After doing this work for twenty years, I've gained a great deal of knowledge about homes and how they change over time: their surfaces and spaces. I have developed efficient methods to achieve a clean home that anyone can do. You can too! Take some time, once you've completed these tasks, to sit down in your favorite spot with a beverage of your choice and savor how rewarding it is to be in your home when it feels this clean.

Taking time to make your home safe, clean, and inviting offers many rewards, so it's worth the effort you give it. Don't deprive yourself of this joy!

Keep your cleaning tools organized and easily accessible in order to make quick clean-ups easy to accomplish at the time a mess occurs. This will make regular maintenance much easier and less time consuming. We all want to spend more time enjoying our clean homes, rather than cleaning our homes.

I wish you luck in your pursuit of clean spaces. Thank you for trusting me to help you achieve this goal. This book may seem to detail a very time consuming task. However, once you learn and practice these methods, tackling them will be a piece of cake.

Regardless of how large or small, or old or new your home is, it is your sanctuary. Treat it as such and savor every moment of your time there. Our home is our respite from the chaotic world around us. I wish for yours to be as clean and comfortable as you deserve it to be.

Thank you for purchasing *Get Your House Clean Now: The Home Cleaning Method Anyone Can Master*. In appreciation, I hope you will utilize my Product Guide to help you find the products I've shared here quickly and easily.

Visit **www.bethmcgeebooks.com/clean-product-guide** to find everything mentioned in this book with easy links to each product. I will be sure to share any new products there that I find to be effective and efficient in cleaning. I hope this resource makes getting your home clean and comfortable that much easier.

If you enjoyed this book, please take a moment to leave a review, so others might benefit from knowing if this information will help them achieve a clean home too. I value and appreciate your feedback. I read every review and use your input to provide a quality experience for future readers. I appreciate your support, dear reader.
Happy house cleaning!

Beth McGee

ABOUT THE AUTHOR

Beth McGee, author of *Get Your House Clean Now: The Home Cleaning Method Anyone Can Master,* is a popular blogger, business owner and community activist who shares her experiences on a number of topics through her writing. She has owned a professional residential cleaning business for over 20 years, helping hundreds of people savor the clean comfort of their homes.

Ms. McGee is author and publisher of the popular blog **MyMobileHomeMakeover.com** where posts and projects give confidence to thousands of visitors a month to turn their manufactured homes into cozy castles, promoting the DIY culture and the value of small and efficient homes. To learn more about Beth McGee and join her list for news and updates, visit: **BethMcGeeBooks.com**

Beth has a bunch of grown children and grandchildren she adores, and enjoys an adventurous life with her husband Darren and their rescue pup Finnegan.

Made in the USA
Monee, IL
09 April 2023

31602818R00075